Changing
on the Fly

Changing on the Fly

The Best Lyric Poems of
George Bowering

POLESTAR
An Imprint of Raincoast Books

Raincoast and Polestar acknowledge the ongoing financial support of the
Government of Canada through The Canada Council for the Arts and the Book
Publishing Industry Development Program (BPIDP); and the Government of
British Columbia through the BC Arts Council.

Editor: Lynn Henry
Cover and interior design: Val Speidel

NATIONAL LIBRARY OF CANADA CATALOGUING IN PUBLICATION

Bowering, George, 1935–
   Changing on the fly : the best poems of George Bowering / George
   Bowering.

   ISBN 1-55192-715-2

   I. Title.

PS8503.O875A6 2004   C811'.54   C2004-901963-5

LIBRARY OF CONGRESS CONTROL NUMBER: 2004092413

Polestar Book Publishers/Raincoast Books
9050 Shaughnessy Street
Vancouver, British Columbia
Canada, V6P 6E5
www.raincoast.com

At Raincoast Books we are committed to protecting the environment and to
the responsible use of natural resources. We are acting on this commitment by
working with suppliers and printers to phase out our use of paper produced
from ancient forests. This book is one step towards that goal. It is printed on
100% ancient-forest-free paper (40% post-consumer recycled), processed
chlorine- and acid-free, and supplied by New Leaf paper. It is printed with
vegetable-based inks. For further information, visit our website at
www.raincoast.com. We are working with Markets Initiative
(www.oldgrowthfree.com) on this project.

Printed in Canada by AGMV Marquis
10 9 8 7 6 5 4 3 2 1

For my sister Sally and my brothers Roger and Jim.

I was a kid in a small town with few streetlights, so I could lie with my back on the grass and watch shooting stars zip across the sky. If I went to the beach at Penticton I could pick up a handful of sand and see grains of ten different colours. I could open the Bible my folks gave me when I was in Grade Three, and read ancient stories about disturbing events.

How could I not write lyric poetry?

I saw a rattlesnake wiggle across our back yard. Wasn't that some kind of poetry being written by someone? Here is the way one becomes a poet: one sees it being done and decides that one wants to do it too. When you're really small you see the bigger kids zipping by on two wheels, and your good sense tells you that it's impossible, that you'll never do it. But you will eventually save up for a two-wheeler, eh?

Just about everybody writes poetry. Young guys at war scribble poems that get found on their bodies. Family members write poems of praise and love for the death notices they put into the classified pages. It's just that most people never try to write better poetry; they don't read books of poems that will teach them how to do it. Even many of the ones that do will drop out early. I have known young poets who wrote the best lyric poetry of our young years, and then went into other lines of work, legal or otherwise.

Young poets tend to write lyrics, and when they get older and prefer to work on longer and more polysemous forms, they occasionally commit a lyric poem that takes two minutes to write and that they will find months later on a piece of paper on the floor. When you are a young poet you might not be clear about what a lyric poem is, except that it has something to do with sounding good accompanied by the poet's fingers on a lyre. M. H. Abrams, who assigned himself the task of defining literary terms for undergrads, said that a lyric poem is "any short poem presenting a single speaker (not necessarily the poet himself) who expresses a state of mind involving thought and feeling."[1] That's not bad for a description that values a combination of terseness and clarity. In fact, I would argue only with the verb "expresses." I hold to the ancient fancy that my poems are permitted from elsewhere, not squeezed from inside.

So here follows a collection of my lyric poems. They have dates on them — that's how it works. Time receives our signatures, and leaves its own on us and our work. These were occasions, as Rilke put it, when the poet was lucky enough to see the visible and the invisible at once.

—GEORGE BOWERING, 2004

---

1   M. H. Abrams, *A Glossary of Literary Terms*, New York, Holt, 1957 p. 48

CONTENTS

AT VICTORY SQUARE

you'll always see
some middle old man
on crutches
        with a gray sock toe
        poking out of a
        strange white cast on his foot

waiting for the traffic light
to somewhere
or else leaning against
the new stone benches
where there used to be
             grass and birds

And you'll always be going
by on a bus
        wondering why
        you dont seem to get down here much
        anymore

till the light changes
and you at least
or maybe both of you

move off

THE BREAD

I saw the bread in the cupboard
and stole
            half a loaf

leaving the bottle of wine
   on the table
       where it belonged

   I left the house
with everybody asleep
  and drove home with it
            stuffed in my coat pocket

Of these things
my present days are made
            moments of larceny
   & charity

FOR A

what joy
to teach you joy
of love

a little
at a time

what fun too
our one
little find
at a time

how dear
the simpleness
of it

how thank you
how thank me

for each
syllable
we say of it

POEM FOR MY WIFE ANGELA

The gardenia
from your wedding day

makes a pouch
in the pages of my
        Shakespeare book

The gray three piece suit
you wore

you wear now
and press on weekends

The gold ring
minted for your finger

is fitted there now
as part of your
        household hours

and your eyes
      of light tears
when you looked at me
        your husband

are part of me too

THE GRASS

I must tell you
of the brown grass
that has twenty times
this year, appeared
from under the
melting snow, reared
its version of spring
like a sea lion coming
out of water, a-dazzle
in the sun, this
brave grass the sun
will only burn again
returning like a tiny
season.

CANADIAN CAFE

The lonely Canadian cafe
at four in the morning

is where I sit
long after the second coffee,

six cents in my pocket,
wind blowing snow around outside.

I keep coming back here
anywhere in the country,

looking for a dead friend
who pretended to love this place.

TEOTIHUACAN

We are sitting on the ancient staircase
smoking cigarettes & just looking
at the grass
in the front yard of Quetzolcoatl

Hey, imagine old feathery Toltecs
up there on the palace, I say
& Angela dreams old dreams
surrounded by square rock walls
the blood all faded off now
no footprints on the ground or face

Behind her, the Temple of the Sun
brown, man-made mountain
quiet in the valley winds
the sun still burning

tanning the face of a little
brown woman, walking towards us
over the broken cobble ground

She wants to sell authentic
Toltec heads cheap, dollar a head

I imagine her years younger
straight & slim, standing
on top of the temple, her chest
bare to the knife, her heart
beating loud for the sun god.

No, gracias, I say now
& she moves away, her face
the same color as the stones

Mexico City / June 25, 1964

THIS HAPPENED AT A MARKET IN THE STATE OF PUEBLA

Imprisoned
in my steel
green Chevrolet

I watcht
her walk by
holding a twine

suspending
three squealing piglets
by their back feet.

She stopt to rest
& the piglets
on the ground

were quiet.
I
was quiet.

*

When you slit
their throats
they are still.

You can work
on them then
carefully.

Calgary / Nov. 27, 1964

CUERNAVACA

Sitting here late morning
at a sidewalk cafe,
toast, coffee, Angela
with half a melon,
inevitable strawberry jam,

camera round my neck
I try to hide,
old personal worn leather
strap round my shoulder,
up high in the eye
a shiny yellow church dome,

I sit still in the shade
not to look like gringo
disappearing in the street
like old Humphrey Bogart
exotic adventure, embarrasst,

but they find me &
shake beads in my face, little
dancing puppets, barata, Señor,
the town going by, old bent
American men, "retired,"

going by with canes &
the American papers, I see one
go by with the paperback of
Fanny Hill. Later we walk
around the town, saying

strange words, "Look at
the Americans," odd people,
walk around with grim face
behind dresst up Mexican
guide, to the palace to the
Diego Rivera mural. Cameras

& grim faces, they never
smile, they are doing a hot
duty, it will be over, they
are the ones with white skin
& the young ones wear white
tennis shoes, this Mexico

is a sporting contest, they
never do anything wrong; we
have finisht our breakfast
& prepare to drive to Mexico.

Mexico City / July 29, 1964

26

RIME OF OUR TIME

Here is Angela's
hair on the side of
my face; love as

clean and soft as
it is immediate
to me. Two heads

on a pillow faces to-
gether eyes closed or
open in the dark.

Time is on our side
now no trick to
scrutinize but behind

us days. Accumulating
sounds we make in
our sleep, our dreams

of one another seen.

F R O S T

But the morning
hoar frost

the breath of cold birds
on trees

the metal of January
in this place.

The crystals, white
hanging from the iron handrail

cold to fingers
sweet to taste.

PRESERVES

Eating preserved pears
this May month

I see the marks of
the paring knife

shape of work
last summer
            preserved

served
working of women in the kitchen

eaten in a minute

THE HOUSE

1.

If I describe my house
I may at last describe my self

but I will surely lie
about the house.

For there is the first lie.
It is not a house at all

but a fragment, a share
of a house, instinct drives me

to one door. As certain as
one hair lies beside another.

As certain as these rows of books
carry me from house to house,

arrange me to their will. I
squat for an hour, eye level

to those books, saying I will
read this, or I will read this,

& this way never succeed
in reading my self, no time

left in the hour between
the news & the pants on the floor.

2.

In the morning the window
is bamboo & behind that

snow. (But here I am trying
to go outside the house, remember

what I said.) My bare feet
find no wood, the water

runs warm from the tap,
the coffee in the white cup

on which is painted a green
tree. There is a newspaper.

on the floor inside the door,
& a woman in the chiffon ·

of the bed. A salt shaker

of glass in an aluminum

pepper shaker, & in the
farthest room, papers, orderly.

Those are the reasons for the house
& its enemy. I am the fisher

who lays his fish side by side
in the pan. The noise of the pen

on paper is the drift of
cigarette smoke in the window's light.

3.

The house has a refrigerator
& a stove, a painting & a

husband, & the husband
has fingers from which words

fall as the wine glass falls
unbroken on the rug.

The key fits into the door
as my feet step in snow, cutting

precise patterns & the silence
of wind, & from outside

the windows are glass, &
behind that the house is not empty.

THE SILENCE

The silence
that some days
brings itself between us

fools my heart,
it thinks there is
a loud constant noise.

THE BOAT

I say to you,
marriage is a boat.

When the seas are
high enough to
turn us over

we must hold
not one another
but our own positions.

Yet when the water
is calm under sea moon

we can even stand up
& dance
holding tight, each to each.

YOU TOO

If you have come this far
you might as well stay,
you might as well be me
for a day.

See my two eyes
if you want to look,
turn my pages, think back,
read the book.

Even marry me, write
my name, you might
as well stay, if I
have come this far.

How can I die alone.
Where will I be then who am now alone,
what groans so pathetically
in this room where I am alone?

I do not know, I know
you begin where my eye
leaves off, you too, turning
my pages are alone.

THE CRUMBLING WALL

A crumbling wall
is a good thing,

it saves a city,
this kind of city,

pushing itself north
wall against new wall.

The foundation
is crumbling, that

is the only way
a community can build.

Let the bricks
fall out. A broken

wall is a thing of
beauty, for a certain

time. Joy does not
last forever. It

requires change, it
must crumble to remain.

A SUDDEN MEASURE

This sudden snow:
        immediately
the prairie is!

Those houses are:
        dark
under roofs of snow —

That hill up to the cloud is:
        markt
        by snow creeks down to town —

This footpath is:
        a bare line
across white field —

        This woman appears
        thru drift of snow:

a red coat.

NOBODY BELONGS

nobody
belongs anywhere,

even the
Rocky Mountains

are still
moving

IS THAT MAN MENZIES LACKING

Is that man Menzies lacking
in imagination?
                    Sits for an hour
in front of some weed,
writing, sketching, rolling paper.

Stops once in a while
to squint at the sun over the sea.

In the southern islands
he sat with his back to the beach palms,
cleaning his quills.

I believe he never thinks
about the king's
northwest passage.

Now he pulls the weed out of the ground
to poke around at its roots.

We'll all go home
the long way, empty-handed
but for my charts
& his weed-book.

THE SOFT AIR OF THE INLAND SEA

The soft air of the inland sea
& heavy spray in the dark spruce
offer no grail, it was no grail
he was after, he was not
sailing with that kind of purity.

He stopped to dine on the silver plates
of the Spanish, Quadra saw no
Celt there, but Vancouver, the reformed
Dutchman, a young sailor
with an appetite.

        As the sea
for its archipelago, wooded islands,
barks with yards wet in the rain,
appetite awakened early, for the
whole world. He sailed
seven days against the tide
thru drifting weed, sputum
of land birds.

        Totem poles
falling in the rain, like Spaniards
in the South, never seen by
land eyes, carry no sail,
the coal underneath, no human bones,

Asiatic footsteps melted ino the
Japanese current, gone home, as
Vancouver, to die early,
to be passed over in favour
of another man, another voyager,
but always re-encountered,
in the names, Japanese & lonely.

LET US SAY

Let us say
this is as far as I, George,
have travelled,

the line
obscured still, the coast
I mean, touched, sighted,
mapped to some extent,
the islands
noted.

Now on this side, east,
it is that much,
water, pines, the Spanish
& their names, the savages
on the edge of water.

I have seen some
of what lies in the mind,
the fancy of the British king
gone like fish odour
into the life-giving fog of that coast.

Aug 2, 1967

ROY IS COVERED

Roy is covered with baubles,
all colours, red jewels
around his neck, red crown
on his long thick blond hair,

sitting on a curious eagle
throne, he displays
what seems a gold flower plate.

(Come on, George, you know the real name, see,
you dissemble already —)

But this royalty
I cant respect, especially sitting.

In school
I was expelled for "sedition." How
can I even name his awe, this mere
hairy king?

(That is the fear made subtle, George,
ask Roy,

> who dissembled even in
> the midst of his vision, even
> in his poem —)

At least this overdressed monarch
shows you his beauteous, empty,
platter,

> the coin of his realm.

I COULD HAVE BEEN ONE

I could have been one
time imagining all this
lying in the sun at Big Sur
real as you can be, but.

               I look in the mirror he holds
& see flowering, he is
               towering over
the green bushes behind him,
                  overpowering
the mirror, a giant coin
           of what realm?

He is one of the few
             not glowering
from his force.
          That force, a weakness
I may overturn with a
           turn of the wrist.

What then of my fear?
The mountains are
                    a distant horizon
I may step over
                to walk away
from them all.
                    Always
walking toward.

            I am imagining all this
real as I can be.

        His grip is gently
on the disc, gentle
                as the flowering
of his soft hat.

SHE IS THE SWEETEST

She is the sweetest young girl,
a mad queen, holding up her wealth,

                            a plate

of gold.

           (I call them plates
           though I know *denier*
           is not to eat from.)

                         She's back
                         in this poem.

An antic one, she
           doesnt know how to carry
               her birthright.

                    So I love her
as I reach back into my days
           on the sun's platter.
               that gold.

She stands awkward
           as if shy to take a stance.
The scepter is correct
           but her head held awkward
& the coin of her realm
           wide open
to the sun's rays.

           Beneath the loose red blouse
        her breasts
        are heavy
with no support
        save her sweet muscles.

The muscles beneath my skull

      respond

      répondez.

SOME DEATHS

My cousin Russell died the night before &
I stayed on the lawn & said I didnt want his
saxophone. It was a death without sex because
he was twenty & I was twelve & we lived twenty-
seven miles apart. In Penticton he played the
saxophone & in Oliver I dreamed of playing the
drums & that dream was dead & that duet was dead
as well & after that I played alone but not the
drums. They offered me the saxophone but I stayed
by myself on the lawn.

My Aunt Dorothy died when I was a baby so
I saw her but mainly in the photograph. She died
of TB where she workt against death as a nurse.
She workt against TB & she died & I never saw
her photograph after I passt the age when she
died & I had my chest photographt to see whether
I had TB.

My grandmother Clara died at Easter & my
grandfather Jabez walkt on his crutches around
the living room saying "Mother" as if she would
not be resurrected. He said it as if she were
his mother, & he an old man. He said it as if
she would not be resurrected & he a former min-
ister of God. It was Easter & the food she had

cookt for the family lay where she left it &
began to undergo the changes brought by death.
Perhaps it was thrown away & perhaps the family
ate it all.

THE GUN

Malediction triggers euthan-
asia. The old poet put quietly to death by a
gun full of bad words. His own the symptoms moving me to action. This happens over & over.

& is not over. Squeeze the trigger. Do not
pull. Do not pull your punches but get it over
as quickly as possible when it seems the kindest
course.

Bad words flow from bad blood. In the far
Orient they are spilling good blood after bad,
the blood of a young poet. What is he doing in
there? Why does the old poet spill his bad words?
Blood flows thru the young finger on the button
in the far East.

The old poet holds the hand that signed the
paper that repairs the house that Jack built.
Jack was not killed with kindness, though the
triggerman cited his bad words. He was felled
when he came out of the woods into the city.

He was no longer in the East & he was no longer young. He was dead. Three little words are easier than three big words. The poet is dead short live the poet.

It is not really moving me to action. It is moving my action. It is in me. Like a bullet or a bad word.

THE CHILDHOOD

She was always asking did you have a happy
childhood & I was always saying a happy childhood I dont know or I suppose so I dont know.
Well she would say would you say you had an unhappy childhood. I dont know I would say an unhappy childhood I guess I would say I had an
unhappy childhood but only for a reason & then
it wouldnt be an unhappy childhood I suppose
you would say. She would say as she was always
saying then what kind of childhood was it really.
I would always say I dont know what kind of
childhood was it really I suppose sometimes it
was happy & sometimes I was unhappy but it was
not unhappy it was that I was unhappy but not
it because even when I was unhappy it was in
all probability happy. She would always be saying then I simply ask you was it or is it a
generally happy childhood or a generally unhappy
childhood. I guess it was all in the way you
look at it for a reason I would say thinking
of her childhood. She wanted to have me ask
about her childhood was it generally a happy
childhood or generally an unhappy childhood
but I would say it depends on the reason you
would want to say whether it was a happy childhood or not.

THE BODY

The body is not muddy it is hardly muddy
it is muscles yes it is still muscles with less
hair at the knee & calf where it has worn pants.
The body is not muddy it has worn places especially the knee & calf where the hair was & is almost gone & there is no hair where the scars
are. There are also parts where the eye can never see & they are not worn by the eye behind
glass & they are worn nevertheless. I am sometimes weary of having worn the body for so long
but I will not say that, goodbye to all that,
so long. So long hair it has been so long, it
has never been so long but it is worn. It was
sweet & sometimes cold. The body is not now nor
has ever been muddy, that is clear. I am in the
middle of a stream & my body is the stream &
what is the boat. The body is not muddy it is
mostly water & so was my mother, she was the
first stream the primal stream I floated out on
to the land I landed on making a bit of mud with
my water. There are parts the eye can not see
because they are in the past they tell us has
done just that, what a view of the stream. If
this is the stream & I am still to float what
is the boat. What is the boat.

GEORGE STANLEY

He comes home from the pub late at night with his back
stiff & the nimbus around his head, Tony Tryyard he is
called & we havent yet learnt the name of his nimbus.

We havent learnt the names of his number so we dont
have his number, his number is not up, he is upstairs
writing for the paper, I can hear him talking on the
phone & I heard him dial a number, a number of them
probably to do with his writing for the paper & because of
that we call him Scoop Stanley & he doesnt like that, in
the daytime he protects his head when his nimbus doesnt.

He is called Tony in the pub & in the paper but at home
we call him Being. Let us call them their names. We are
the other two & we are called Nothingness & And. This
is a story that goes round & round. Heidegger told this
story & Dorn who had not heard that story told it &
we who had not heard that story or that story told it &
we still tell it. We tell it. Tony's other names.

Names & numbers. He moves from one to the other thru
the door of flesh & there loses his nimbus till he needs it.
He is a friend for whom all have their names. I dont know
when the number is 1 & the name is I, that is when the
name is presumably 1, but in his case I am not I so I
would not know.

b p NICHOL

I walkt to the back of the house in the
yard near the garage & saw him in a
white shirt playing ping pong with a patient
or friend or someone else who lived in the
house & there he was.
I sat at the table where we were reading
aloud together & heard him from behind where
he was crying aloud & wearing his pink
leather number on the west coast & I
must tell you he is a star.
Maybe Holofernes.
He tried to grow a mustache & took his
vacation in a classy hotel in Bermuda where
he sat & drank bourbon with ice, a poet
taking his own kind of holiday, hooray.
Judy lookt as if she wanted to be him
or be with him or kill him.
I think that all the time he was listening
to the ice in the glass his ear was thinking
ping
pong
ping
pong
pingngngngng
One time he placed a bottle of Pinch on the
coat hook on the back of the door in our

clothes closet & we opened & closed the door
for two months before we found the bottle
of Pinch & it should have fallen off many
times so we drank it & later I bought him
a bottle of Pinch in August because the night
before we had been drinking bourbon on his
credit card in the bar where he goes to
drink his own way, the poet.
There he was, on the tape, all over the
country, making personal appearances, Captain
Poetry, listening to the voices of the four
horsemen in the children's fiery
chamber of verse.

DAPHNE MARLATT

In the midst of her sorrow she was
pisst off.
    I always thought if I ever took her
wrist between my finger & thumb it might
snap. But that she can get pisst off, & in
her writing.
    I always thought the words snapt from
her one by one, twigs the birds rested
on & when they flew someone snapt them
off.
    But inside her head there is a torrent. It
is enough to step into that & bathe.
    (In the bath she must be remarkable among
the white porcelain

                 & what does she do with
that long wiry black hair with white strands
running thru?)
    Lately the sorrow is no longer borne & her
body is discovered not to be brittle & her
voice tells you she is pisst off but it has a
little too much humour in it, a thin strand of
that, inside out sorrow.
    In 1960 she had black pedal-pushers & she
lookt so brittle I thought how does she move her
knees, is it painful, & then in 1965 the poems —

how could you follow them without breaking
your tongue.

Even then no one knew she was pisst off,
she didnt know because women didnt really
know & she made poems that were questions
stretcht out in space, ready to be snapt off.

Now you should hear her shout. It
is as if a stick had come alive in your hand.

JAMES REANEY

He is walking over the wooden bridge on
the street in his home town, his soft shoes
& soft feet on the bridge & his head in
black space between stars on either side
or is it totally white space a white space
that is all stars or all star no colours in
the dark & now he has finisht walking over
the bridge.
    That was in a movie or some of it, here
I am back again, the words, they wont leave
you alone, they are opaque but you can see
thru them or the beginning of the passage. Pass.
    All right. He is behind the screen of the
puppet stage holding the strings & is he sur-
prised to feel life coming up along them, that
tug, or is he fishing. Ocean has its own
life its own mountains a starfish for every
star in the sky. His head is there among the fish
& he is swimming, a James undersea for the James
with soft shoes on the ground, this is a good one
because I didnt put that there, the shoes of the
fisherman. Old Jacob. The usurper. I mean where
does the rain come from the provider, the
flood, it is only going home every six months
& where would that go if he didnt pull on the
line, to begin another.

There he is, in the river, wondering what
its name is because some of it is running thru
him, a drink in the, in the

      moment that just went by. If your head
is between the stars of unwavering light it is
a large head, large enough & round enough
to contain the dark & the whiteness con-
tending, large enough to let it be & to feel
the tug that produces colours for the earth
you see when you step off the end of the bridge.

THE BIGAMIST

Dont be angry with your husband the bigamist.
I was married to Death before I knew you.
She lay with me when I was a child.
After the age of consent I was too tired to seek a divorce.
Now you lie with both of us in our bed, our flesh is one.
Her life depends on my first wedding.
Your body is my flower, hers is my sad bright sun.
There is no impediment to the marriage of our minds, no
estrangement because she is my mother & my flesh.
You too are the mother of death, & her lover.

FEET, NOT EYES

How I got close to the prairie. Or realized it.
This was in Manitoba, 1955. I had got loose all
alone & a little drunk hitchhiking west on One
between The Peg & Portage about ten miles west
of city edge, a totally starless night, low clouds
I imagined, & no other light because no farm-
houses. It is an absolute straight highway & my
measurement, my feet feeling pavement or
gravel at the edge, back & forth, my coat hanging unbuttoned, I actually wavered like a movie
drunk along the hard surface, till I stopt &
stared I thought straight upward. There were
no stars & no moonlight could get thru or
around those clouds, & when I felt my way to
the edge of the hard surface I knew I could
look five miles in either direction to see head-
lights but there were none. Nowhere in the imagined
fields around me was there any bird
noise or animal grunt, no wind to move grass
or scraps of paper thrown from car windows
& presumably faded from rain & sun. There
could have been a mountain in its own darkness
creep up & stop five feet from me, but I thought
there was none. I knew I stood on the flatland,
my head in the air or maybe the sky, & in all
directions the darkness was equal & equal the

distance. My only touch was thru the thick shoes
to the surface but that could not keep me long
from falling. This was the dark of the prairie,
& I will never lose the portion that came into
my head & found its place just as full.

FIRST NIGHT OF FALL, GROSVENOR AVE

In the blue lamplight
the leaf falls

on its shadow

FALL, AGAIN

The leaves
dropping on the sidewalk.

I thought
they were footsteps

behind me.

DERELICTS IN THE METRO STATION

He walks in-
tently
to the
waste basket

making it
look like his
job.

DID

One thousand icebergs
in the sunlight around
the corner of New-
foundland, I saw

from the window
of a VC 10.
& wisht William Blake
could have seen that.

I did,

he said.

NEW LOVE

This is the kind of Christmas I like,
thin persistent rain on everyone,
a smasht abandoned English car
across the street, hockey games ruining
all their plans.

        I'd like to spend
Christmas day with John Newlove,
drinking rum & coke in front of
the TV set, watching Paul Warfield
dropping a perfect pass.

        I'm not
kidding, dont ask me why, asking
me why is the worst part of
the Yule Season. I'd like to spend

a hundred dollars & all day
a month after Christmas bringing
unexpected cheer & radiant packages
to all my friends, shouting ho ho,
stomping snow & emptying
Norways of delicious cakes
in front of their startled
& uncomprehendingly beautiful eyes.

STUCK WASPS

It's the end of summer
at the PNE

the cotton candy booth
is full of wasps

half of them flying
half of them stuck

The two candy women
have given up —

God, what a fresh image

God, what a cynical poet

Do you want pink or blue?
I'll have blue, said Thea

That'll be 75¢
said the candy woman
with the blue

SCRAPING IN ITALY

In Florence, Tusc
on Christmas day
my wife was at the sink.

So I had to shave
in the bidet,
& that set me to think:

did Giotto too,
did Cimabue
improvise, & feel the course of wit
as they bent to wash a brush?

Wash, that is, a male brush
held in fingers imagining
a gold halo while
scraping at only flesh?

A PRAYER

Lord God

if I have but one life to live,
I hope this aint it.

AGAINST DESCRIPTION

I went to the blackberries
on the vine.

They were blackberries
on the vine.

They were
blackberries.

Black
berries.

WEST WINDOW

grip down & begin to awaken

The tendril that grew last spring across my study window
is now a bare branch.

                              I dont recall being hugged
by either of my parents; I grew that way, food in my
mouth they gave me, frequent drinks of water,
exercise in the hills behind the house
& in the back yard. They made certain I had
work to do there.

I dont remind myself of anyone in my family,
the greedy way I am always hugging my daughter,
smoothing her hair while she sleeps. I would rather
watch her than watch her grow,
                    but she does. & I put food in her mouth.

Now a bare branch. I have often told myself
to cut it down, it is a creeper like a weed, cut it down
& while you are at it, rake last summer's leaves
now frozen to the lawn. But I dont do it, day after day,

& after doing it just this once more,
dont make any more figures in which you compare
foliage & children.

WHICH POESY

Thou many-coloured, many-voicèd vale,
over whose pines, & crags, & caverns sail
fast cloud shadows & sunbeams, art an
agreeable place, Chamonix, made of tired wood,
a mountain outside the toilet window.
An agreeable place, I love you, the strange sleep
which when the voices of the desert fail
wraps all in its own deep eternity.
On the walk back to our pension
I overtook a tiny old Frenchman who sang
in the dark bending street, an old romantic
French song, his soul flowing from his small lungs
to the mountaintop somewhere high above him
in the clouds. Whose wandering wings
now float above thy darkness, & now rest
where that or thou art no unbidden guest,
in the still cave of the witch Poesy.

2.

I lookt from the window of our poor pension,
to the sun rowdy & confident at home
there in the mountains. The snow all year
lies shining over its melting self. I stare:
has some unknown omnipotence unfurled
the veil of life & death? Or do I lie
in dream?
              An Indian jet smasht into that peak
two months ago, an unbidden thought, but I
lookt & traced a trajectory where in one
second a 707 turned nine hundred into zero.

Nearby the lower slopes are grassy, cows nibble
about the camera, bells tinkle, the glaciers creep
like snakes that watch their prey, flowers
wave their hats, steep cablecars rise
on every side — recently one line snapt,
strewing corpses down the glistening slope.
These mountains only stand, quiet in the light,
& men kill themselves all over their sides,
& their place is not known.

3.

Mont Blanc yet gleams on high — the power is there,
the memory rolls thru space & summons
home, the trees into which the roads push
are pines, we grew among them. The snows descend
upon that Mountain; none beholds them there,
nor when the flakes burn in the sinking sun,
or the star-beams dart thru them.

A man
doesnt drive a car under a mountain every day.
It is cool inside Europe's highest mountain,
beneath considerable masses of rock & earth.
The road is unusually straight for the Continent,
over eleven kilometres in length. But
if to the human mind's imaginings
silence & solitude were vacancy, this
painted line across the pavement would be
the Italian border, the road would now
slope downward, the air would be warm
as the first breath of your baby.

ARTAUD'S HAIR

They cut Artaud's hair
      before they buried him,
carved a death study
      like a prime minister.

Headless, or a head alone,
      the centre of madness
where Artaud lived during
      Hitler's sane ravage of Europe.

His hair grew longer than the teeth
      of Winston Churchill,
the loose legs of Franklin Delano Roosevelt,
      the bombs of Dresden.

In the madhouse Artaud's hair
      fell softly,
            softly.

MY FATHER IN NEW ZEALAND

Everyone agrees,
when you visit New Zealand
you are back in the Fifties.

The Fifties! My father is still alive!
I looked around for him on the long main street of
      Wellington.
I kept turning on Cuba Street to see if he was behind me.
I listened for his quiet voice in the Auckland airport.
I lifted brims of bent sheepmen's hats, looking for his face.

He was there somewhere, I had no right
to wander both islands without talking to him.

I rued the hours I spent in the wrong places,
the Vibrations disco in Christchurch, the Maori bars,
the poetry reading at the library. He
would never show up in such a place, and my time
was running out.

Every time I watched a flashing leg
instead of seeking his dear old frame
I was suffused with guilt, a true Canadian abroad.

Dear Ewart, if they are right you are there somewhere,
& I have twenty years to find you
before you are gone again, maybe to some other country.

But how many years do I have left, whose frame
looks so much like yours? Can I wait twenty years,
hoping you move to a closer country?

Are you in New Zealand, looking for me too?
I am a lot older now, I look more like you.
Call me by the secret name we had when I was a child,
the name we never spoke. I'll hear you if I can get there.

JUST AS WE LOSE

Just as we lose the last innocence
one comes to tell us there's more;
her date of birth is unimaginable,
no one has seen her before.

Goodness and mercy are such temptations,
love is a bear in the street;
all our old friends are resting their angers,
shuffling their cards and their feet,
shuffling their hands and their feet —
calling off war with the last of our innocence
one swaggers down to defeat.

READY TO SNAP

Ready to snap, he focuses
on infinity, holds his finger,
yes, holds his nerve, gives a

Kiss to the quick singer
in your ear. He's recorded
your soul. He's painted your face
on silver. Shine back
on his open eye your instant grace,
kiss him in a glance
ask his wide eye to dance.

H

      is the favourite letter
of my favourite poet. Hello there,

and Help me, will you, nobody
knows my name, and they all
know your initials.

Would you write me a letter
of introduction. Dear fave,
help me now and in the Hour
of my greatest reading. You
Have the Hours, a book
few people read and fewer
write.

Soon,

      Mother
or an   other
organ

·

O

round, O
world, where On your sure face
will I find the bend
            that bends for me?

The be all and end all;
the ball bounces more than Once,
and I bounce On it, wondering

where O where
will the circle become square,
the bend all flat,
where I'll know, O where I'm at?

I'm bound,
On my way
but all tied up.

I've never found,
never have I found dead
what was Only started,

nor found a live
ending, a live O.

I've wanted to be low
where the sure face
would never be turned
to ward me
Off.

V

for Vic Tory you thought,
laying on the liberal
Varnish,
        till I be
came here today gone to
morrow.

        Your shining's
tar. Politics and star-making
never were your long
suits.
        (How I hated your clothes.)

        Just this side
of celestial bodies
I was Vanished, like a V
of wild geese, and you,

you were just the north.

D E A T H

I'm going to write a poem about life & death, I said, but
mostly about death. But you are always doing that, said D,
your last poem was about death. The poem before that one
was about death. In fact if you looked at all your writing,
especially the poems, you would find pretty near nothing
but death. A lot of the time you seem to be laughing about
it, but that doesnt fool anyone.

Yes, but this time I am going to make it a real poem about
life but mainly death, I'll grant you that. None of that lacy
Rilke death, non of that ho ho Vonnegut death. I mean real
death or I should say real thinking about death. For instance?
asked D. Well, for instance, take the way you feel like how
awful it will be when you cant put an arm around a waist,
long arm the way it is just made to snake around a perfect
waist, & there is that swelling out of hip upon which it is
natural to rest an arm. How wonderful, and how terrible not
to be able to look forward to that ever again.

You see? said D, you announce that you are going to say
something straight about death, and there you are talking
about life, as far as I can see. That's just my point, I said.
Death will be horrible because it wont have anything of life
in it, no matter how many fancypants graduate students
have told me that you cant really submerge yourself in life

unless you are fully conscious of your death. They have all been reading Albert Camus lately, & they are so much wiser than I am.

I suppose you are using all the things I have been saying as part of your poem, said D. Of course, I said. You are to this poem as a swelling out of lovely hip is to an arm that has snaked around a dear waist.

Just then I realized that I had made D up in my imagination, & now there was no D at all, & I had to forget about writing another poem about life & death but especially about death, especially about death from a straight point of view, because M came into the room while I was typing & had a persistent gripe about C, & no matter how interrupted I managed to make myself look on the chair in front of the keyboard, M just kept on & on till the poem had followed D to some place we will never find the way to.

MY FAMILY'S ALL IN BED

I'm up
against the silences to come   .

They keep telling me to talk more,
write less —

but I cant figure this out, I
will be doing neither
soon enough   .

                              And think
when the ears that hear me talk are dead
I'm done forever
talking   .

                    But someone,
dear descendent,
might read a page out loud
in the twenty-first century,
her familiar time —

and there I'll be (no book, etc)
where neither you nor I can hear me

But closing the book, someone
will close my words on each other,

maybe these I'm writing in a lorn kitchen,
dark January outside,
a lot of silence in this place   .

THE DRIFT

In Canada, he said, you have
a nuclear winter every year,
but the sun always, he said,
comes back, and you have
another wheat harvest.

                          The gift,
I figure, of the magi.

You will follow a star
if there is no sun. A moth
will aspire to Venus
if he cant find a flame.

So Christmas. It comes to Flin Flon
when Flin Flon, I mean for example,
needs it. A Canadian winter,
the one they show me on billboards,
is no idyl, the god of snow
does not fiddle, no cow I know
can jump from the foothills
over the moon.

2.

This is the month, and this
the happy morn, he said. Yes
and the unhappy are filled
with jubilation. It depends

like a full stocking off a fireplace
mantle, it depends. Do you see
the death of winter born
with the deepest December snow?

Do you see that billboard,
deep tire tracks in the white,
a Canadian winter — it's
expensive. We know who's filled

with jubilation. Every winter
is new and every midnight is clear,
and someone has to pay
for those long tall magnesium candles

cuddled in their electronic silos,
round yon virgin, under the drift
of dry snow, belly deep in
the collected blood of the roast lamb.

3.

And then, they said, no spirit can walk abroad,
Flin Flon, hunkered at our heart, is sure,
its fires burn friendly molecules, some god
we celebrate clenches us, like a young woman
in a Japanese car, before the heater kicks in.

The night is wholesome, no planets strike.
Our friendly fire burns till dawn,
while north of us the Dew Line rots away.

No fairy tales, nor witch has power to charm,
so sacred is the time, so gracious,
so forgetful are we, so loud did Santa
roar from his disguised motor
on the bare pavement, in the mall.

She's a schoolteacher, that's why
she's in that Japanese car. It is
almost new. It is driving along
one of the cross-hairs on a distant scope,
but she doesn't know that.

She thinks it is the invisible
Saskatchewan border. She can see lines of lights
that are winter roofs
in Manitoba.

4.

What harvest?
What gift?
What magi?

In a drear-nighted December, he said,
too happy, happy tree,
your branches dont remember
their green felicity.

The tree, the tree, the Christmas
tree cut down dead, Jesus
come down, the old decorations
go back up, the star no sun on top.

The tree, dying slowly, like a world,
is covered with shiny
petroleum products, magic for the very young,
goodbye for a pine
that never will be.

This the happy never morn,
they'll chuck him over the fence,
brown in the back lane, crisp
in the wet snow; never count the rings,
his age, never see
the invisible god, never evergreen.

5.

If winter comes, he might say,
spring can be so far behind,
she'll never catch up.

If winter comes upon a midnight
new and clear, even Mr. Flin Flon
will not have time

to remember Satan, on his motor,
on the soft pavement, in the mall,
waving his bright red arm
at them all.

A sad song, a carol
at every doorstep.
We do need the time, this dark afternoon,
to sleep in earthly peace.

We do need you, sleeping child,
we do need you, soil asleep
beneath a brittle snow.

We do need you, poets of the seed,
stacked in the warm shed,
waiting for an ancient sun.

We need you, too, you unnameable,
blow the flame off your candles,
climb out of that warm concrete hole,
put your heart's gloves on,

give us two hands, help us
push this little Japanese car
out of the drift.

MUNICIPAL STADIUM 1988

It should have been my father that was here,
he a Cleveland Indians fan for no known reason,
no geography —
                    only major league game he saw
was in Montreal, 1970.

                    Here the Mistake by the Lake,
nearly empty, or seven thousand good-natured souls
against the ever-present Kansas City Royals.

To show my skill I boo Bill Buckner, .241,
for insisting on wearing a glove in the '86 Series.

My companions were born to this;
I had to earn it, a boy in Okanagan sand,
now sitting in baseball's biggest park,

old as the century, old as the league, old
as Hart Crane, throw me a lifesaver.

My companions and I had ethnic sandwiches
in a real U.S. bar, sports photos on the wall.

They respect me, they want to know
what I can tell them. I sit in that old yard

and celebrate. I made it here. I think of my Dad,
and act unlike him, exactly,
loud mouth, cheering the Tribe,
sardonic, in love, broken in the ball park.

MUSINGS ON SOME POETS

Those poets, heads coming out of collars,
advised us, showed us how to hold paper and look good,
did we sometime grow tired of them, those
who lived for us,
died for us,
rotted under ground for us,
are still
so we may move.

Not friends, really, not teachers,
poets, whose names glittered when we were alone,
whose books dropped like gleaming newborn calves into
    our unsteady hands,
did we read them as if pulling shavings off our souls,
never stepped out of the Pacific combers with shine on
    morning face,
never twisted body out of grip of coal giant ogre
save with inspiration of our poets,
and who knows what our
means?

What are we now besides older;
a young man newly graduated from university,
black gown still on him said I envy you and your friends,
you got to make the last ones,
there isnt anything to make now, or no one knows what
    there is.
I said it seems that way but there is always something,
and I showed him my teeth through yellow beer.

Do we old farts say thank you every genuflecting morning
to those poets with agate names who showed us their
    synapses?
Nowadays the young want us to love the earth,
And I never say out loud to them that my dear old people
Are columns of earth, walk around, sit in chairs,
discard cigarettes and write that's left of poems.
They were low lights between mountains visible
to the evening gaze, they were evaporate mornings,
They are not mulch but stones in the earth, they are not
specimens but the authors of words should be whispered
    inside a dark bowl from Siena.

I have no remaining skill for form,
just feel words jostle each other in doorways on the way
        out, sit here this
evening remembering a former life, I'm with friends
all lovely all restrained by hope, all agreed without saying so
— those poets gave us a way to waste our lives
saying useless things, smiling indulgently at each other's
        personal diaspora,
carrying mismatched goodies on the way to the grave,
trip, fall into hole, write on dirt walls,
a first and last sonnet,
solving all, coming to rest, combing hair, adjusting socks,
kissing no one but the image of Jesus, disbursing mind as if
        it were mercury,
listening for the voices to arrive with the worms.

MISS HIM

Mister Audio had a ball while he was here, or at least he tossed it to us, and as it bounced we sang, naughty boys in the dark theatre.

Mister Odeon flashed a light in the dark rows looking to see whether we were having fun for our five cents, multifoliate as all get out.

Mister Completely told the worst jokes he could think of, his poems full of holes like a house coat he was not oriented to, what a get up.

Mister Dressup wore shirts and pants made by Missus like crazy, he was the man with the golden throat, velour tonsils you would say.

Mister Poetry got his commission, got his promotion, made captain and the kids loved him like crazy, stuck to him like glue.

Mister Big grew like a long poem, a page at a time, boy did he have crazy hair, always a pencil in it, always writing home, starting with H.

I —
mmmm
rrrr

Missed a few lines there, must be one of those holes, my guess is — he's in there exactly, Señor Duende, here with us today in this brave dream.

FILL OUR HOUSES

Every time Roy Kiyooka came back from somewhere he was wearing some shoes no on else ever had.

Roy Kiyooka had small feet and small hips and a big forehead and a few chin hairs and two missing finger tips.

His body was so small it could have been fitted inside his enormous laugh.

Oh dear, he would say at the end of that laugh, and m-hmm, m-hmm, as he returned to whatever he had been saying.

Once he laughed and said oh dear all the way down the 401 in a drive-away car from Montreal to Toronto, sometimes a little off the pavement.

He hardly ever looked through the windshield. I was in the back seat and he was looking at me. Scared me to death.

Guys like me will never understand Zen and hokku and hard edge ellipses, but we fill our houses with them.

Fill our houses with Roy Kiyooka, walk by him every day from now on, catch sight of a head band.

My keyboard always spells it Kiyooks. I have to correct it every time. I've written Kiyooks and Kiyooka five thousand times in my life.

Nevertheless, these ears would lend anything to hear that waterslide laugh again, ten more times.

We've all got him, Roy. Never saw so many friends. Students coming out of the walls. Family on the moon.

I lost my favourite old shoes around the time Roy was leaving us. I'd let them go forever if I could spend a life with old Kiyooks.

THE GREAT LOCAL POEM

The great local poem begins
when someone pulls

out the last spike.

We declare the hole that is left
the centre of everything.

FALL 1962. VANCOUVER

Inside the strangeness of living
as a young man, with.

With A, they went to see his
soppy hero, nearly jazzman, Sammy
Davis Junior, at the Queen.
Elisabeth Theatre. It was very nice
to see him at last, gratifying
to hear him do Frank Sinatra
the white guy.

Snow. C. P.
Snow sees the continent of the rich
pull away from the continent poor.

We need, he says, to revampire
western education, supply money, send
men to poor lands, prod
their revolutions. China, 1949.

But intellectuals. They are rooted
in the so far
all right soil of the past. They do impressions
(if you want unity) of the past. This
is tradition. Not the strange.

SPRING 1967. LONDON

Snowing and melting, central
Canaday is March, time to read, he said,
the Fried North Throwup poets, Le
Pang! , Mac
Person! , James Rain
Man! , but hey, this one's pretty
good!

Time, he said, to go to the
York!, sit in on
drums! with the Nihilist Spasm
Band!

          Yor k-no good,
they said, keep slipping
into time.

          And away
to another bar where two drunken men
walk into the women's toilet.

And outside in Ontario
it is snowing out the night sky,
you should be home
standing in right field.

Poem? You can
finish it

[   ]

This is tradition,
not the strange.
She makes good use
of the NY *Times* cook book he got
as introduction to that book club. He's
getting a belly

full. "B
reveals that it's easier to write
poems about nothing than it is to write
short stories about nothing."

Ian Dunn died on the highway
ten years ago, his funeral last night
occurred in a cave. When he was
carried in I saw his head bobbing.
Etc.

Little Gumpy,
with her small stem glass,
has become something of an expert
wine fancier,

a short story becoming more familiar
with time.

WINTER 1981. VENICE

Here beside this dark sea
the dainty *Doge* has scrambled indoors.

How lucky they were yesterday
to see snow in St Mark's square,

how lucky today to look out their window
on people in hip waders
carrying widows across the riva.

At five-thirty in the morning
he woke to hear Italian shouted below,

from mature throats. Yesterday in the Basilica
the children's choir faltered
when the parents' applause
greeted the Cardinal's entrance from off-stage.

Later outside, the liberated boys and girls
were learning to make snowballs.

This, he told his daughter,
is what happens when you marry the sea.

SPRING 1984.
TORONTO / VANCOUVER

In the fireplace room at Ithaca
where there was church there was

Curious, friends to see in Ontario,
fuel to pump into wings,

metric measure to remember. Sarah
insisted on spelling her name Saraht

because she loves T as her father
adores H, a letter or ladder

to a Higher place. Fire from
these wings? Hope keeping us aloft,

an H in the heart, he says smugly,
a daughter to fate, his holding

a chocolate T last Christmas, all these
private visits he loves and readers

stand or dont. The craft, to be plain,
looks new, not many riders in it, flying

from snow to know, he cannot kneel
but he adores you, daughters, he wings

on by your inquisitive smiles.

SUMMER (WINTER) 1988.
CANBERRA

He loves them, he loves
being with them, his dear Aussies,
an A in the heart. They care
for each other, they fly from
know to yes.

A long way from home
at the end. It happened that way. A
peacock in the snow would be fine,
a plane crumpled in a forest. Exploded words
catching fire, classical relation
ship in you poem, maybe.

A curious peril,
the gods have in mind, Küsnacht
will look prosperous and lonely, a
woman walking with him will resemble
a ghost.

But here in Canberra it is
midwinter already. They eat outdoors at long tables.
The movie gets ghastly at the end
but it isnt
the end.

PALE BLUE COVER

In the middle of the night Matt would fly to Vancouver so
    he could take a walk on the sea wall the next day, then
    go home.
Wouldnt tell anyone, no telephone call, just run a scene
    through his peculiar Ontario head, no snow on that
    beach.
No one can imagine Matt teaching religion at McMaster,
    Matt eyeing math in a Bay Street shop window.
Here's the man expecting every book to be the break-
    through to best seller Toronto, Spanish doctors
    couldnt even do it.
English patients could do it, Spanish doctors, get out of
    town. Spanish girls, you can forget it.
Matt was planning to write a hundred novels, line them up
    like matched jewelry, strike a shovel into the heart of
    bony Canada.
Mix a metaphor, wrestle a fish in a northern river, propel
    prose like nobody's business, business had nothing to
    do with it.
In the middle of the day Cohen was a wry anglo saxon
    typing on a rocky farm, two thousand words before
    supper.
Remain wry, people like me catch you lost in thought down
    there at the other end of the table, face turned to the
    corner with imagination in it.

We remind ourselves of this undreamable sephardic rock
  agriculturalist, shovel bouncing off some kind of
  precambrian anapest.
He really thought he could get across Canada, get over the
  twentieth century, pick the whole country up and turn
  it over.
No on will ever know what he was thinking on the red-eye,
  patriot satyr grin on his lip.

WIRE WHISK, ELBOWS

He's your New York soul made visible by a patina of
pulp mill, bleaker than Bleecker, heavier than air, sweet as
Keely Smith.

He's really the piano player, I said this in my sleep, but
someone's got to play drums, ting ting ting padaráp.

Looks good in a parka, he has to be hiding from
something, and then there's that mustache, most of the time.

He makes poetry out of politics and no one does either
of them better, but who's listening, have you heard that
before?

His voice has irony hard-wired now, dont tell me
about the new millennium, nothing's new, ask Barry.

Jump for Joy, that was the name of an old album,
probably Dave Brubeck, were you ever in this world?

Lots of guys in New York wear parkas, it's a big town
with small town stuff all over, but you cant leave footprints
in Gotham.

I'd follow him anywhere in Prince George, he dont
scare any harder than I do, and I want to be around his
humour.

Did I say politics? I meant music. And politics, too.

LADDERS, NO SNAKES

I took a sharp right and drove to the house of
F. R.Scott, who offered Allen a famous martini.

Now I live two doors from Warren's house, where
Allen won all the Monopoly® games, and offered no
cheap rent.

Houses cost a lot on Boardwalk.

He lifted the roof of the house on his lap, and out
came music, a drone like his voice.

Outdoors he would sit on a railroad track or a Chicago
street, a blessing on both your houses.

Today he is in the house of the Lord, which is all
around us — Jacob dreamed that for us.

The House Unamerican Activities Committee is never
home, they're on the road, looking for Ginsbergs.

F. R. Scott wrote socialism in Saskatchewan, and Allen
Ginsberg knew it in New Jersey.

Warren came from Washington, poets rime like crazy,
ask Allen, sunflower at his side, ask him.

He'll tell you my house is your house, take your shoes
off, make some popcorn, Hare Krishna, abide forever.

GUN SHY

A Canada without Quebec would stumble through to somewhere this side of the ocean, open to love, helpless over here.

A Canada without him would have no brain but only landscapes sung endlessly by warblers with white corpuscles galore.

He's number one on my bookshelves, look no further, a brain full of muscles, a beach of a continent not yet imagined.

He is this book not often enough, from hour to hour, day to day; as long as he does not commit suicide he has no intention of stopping.

A Canada without him would have a hole in its memory, a space to fall through, a true catastrophe, a sneeze for eternity.

A Canada without him was his dearest wish, and we who feel saved by his brain must turn and say goodbye over and over.

Armed violence is missing in our life, and so is our wild triumph, our thousand attempts to leave, our silence notwithstanding.

A quintessential moment in the Hotel d'Angleterre, an incident without report, a gunshot no one ever heard, a foretelling in every book, now that it is too late, we see them clearly coming.

They are in the near future, less than twenty years ago, and so is our greatest novelist at last, who will not live in our country.

He is born every time we sit down to write but he will refuse to read us, caught in a history that never happened.

O bomber! spare us and take us where you are, dead among the dead, a can of nitro-glycerine in either hand, in a key-stroke country we can all renounce together.

RED HAIR? REALLY?

I saw him when he was old and skinny, with a wheelbarrow full of weeds and broken glass in Lionel Kearns's back yard, a terrific house guest.

Fifteen years earlier he almost ran over me in his red Volvo sports car at Bay and Bloor.

But the only poet who ever ran over me was Lionel Kearns, five years before that, with his Mini Cooper.

Earle. In his creative writing seminar everyone was going to bed with everyone else, or into the back seats of their cars. Those that had cars.

He liked having good-looking young people in his creative writing seminars. It was always very lyrical.

No one ever pushed anyone else off a mountain cliff, we had sore backs, that's all, Earle had a beard, so did Lionel Kearns, so did Frank Davey.

His biographer said he had a big dick, but I never saw it, couldn't tell you, but I've seen some poets' dicks, nothing unusual.

Earle wrote poems in wax, on steps, on mobiles, in the sand. He wrote poems for falling out of trees and airplanes.

The mountains we never fell off are still there, they'll be around, nearly as long as Earle was. He was a cartesian mountain boy, or a goat, he was a mountain.

SILVER AND GOLD,
THE FLOOR OF NIGHT

She can paint a garden so terribly Irwinesque you
want to levitate so you wont squash a Martian tendril.

A martini would be nice with a sprig of that in it, clear
liquid you might see a scary smile through.

Her vestal sweethearts lost their innocence when she
put a brush to paper, a fingernail to the poem, but they
smile like a Joe Rosenblatt cat.

They make us buffoons want to say let's have a peek,
eh, Page, and instantly regret our lives to date.

Is she woman? Or bird? What secret colour is the
lining of her mouth? What was her address on Mars,
anyway?

I think she is a bird. Have you seen those eyes when
they are wide open, looking at you? Did you ever crouch to
the ground, an owl overhead?

Did you ever seek refuge in rime, knowing that the
distant mountain will never be near enough?

A martini would be nice, a stiffener before the rapture,
a liquifying of the throat for your last song before her
words lift you into the night.

SUMMER SOLSTICE

I

The cool Pacific spring has gone without
my notice, now summer lies around us
once again. How long life is, how many
more of these seasons must I see, hydrangea
& the fat rhododendron sullen on the
neighbour's lawn. & I must rise, stick
fluid in mouth, stick beaten vegetables
into my living daughter's mouth, shit, it comes
& goes, it goes, thru us pretending we are
not some more, shit, the wearisome sun
& the sad motes in its visitations envelop
my mind even when it is thinking action
& when it thinks offers impatience with this
boring reappearance of the grass.

II

                              Must I
live longer year by year, watching from this
small mountain the heavier pall of sludge
residing over this city & the yet discernible
waterways of bygone sea manoeuvres, my baby
breathing under that? Every midnight, every

winter, removing familiar clothes & taking
others more familiar to my bed of habit?

III

What nature gave me at my birth no more
than this, a prospectus of recurring faces, old
leaves appear above ground, old words grow
to surround them, old fingers join to pull
them & cast them to their home.

IV

The grass needs cutting, part of it
is yellow, it is dying of starvation, hell
it will be back next year, somewhere
else, & so will we, will we? Will
we endure that? The Pacific winter remembered more fondly than it is, some
unconvincing refuge of the life-giving
horror felt in the knives of Quebec December.
We congratulate each other for the snowy
re-emergence of the mountains, our mountains
we say with fancy dinners at the top
& hydroelectric sticks poking up the
slopes, our mountains re-emerging from our

papermaking smoke, our mountains showing up
each year with their peaks capt, silent
& gentle, the air restful over them, the sea
content to lie beneath them, not looking
for any entrance to that stilled heart.

v

It is slowly dying, but so slowly, the
earthquake belt is forty miles west, the sea
deterred by that long island. Every summer's
pollen mixt with more haze. We come
back here to partake of slow death, the dying
ocean so lifelike, harder to beat down than some
great lake. The mountains once promist me
a rapid death, fall is a fall, to the
rocks below — but the mountains are some-
body's back yard, hydrangea bushes all round.

VI

I havent heard a timely utterance for a
long time, there we are, hung on those
hands, watching & watching, & will they
never move? We seek out ways of death,
but slowly, or given minimal expectation, why

do I climb those stairs every morning?
To visit her, lift her eighteen pounds, &
clean her, more of it she'll pass & never
recall, to bring her downstairs for more,
of the same. Some will say that is reason
enough. Few will say enough of reason. It's
not reason I seek upstairs, we ought to be
past that, it's legs take us up there, legs
more tired every season. She makes utterances
we measure her time by.

VII

Sunday, I & Thea were there when Angela
woke up. So I'm back, she said, &
reacht to touch her baby's fuzzy head. Why,
where have you been, I ask her.

I went on a car ride with a Fairie,
name of Mab.

What did she tell you?

She said things are going to get better.

VIII

I am slowly dying, water evaporating
from a saucer. I saw my daughter this
morning, trying to walk, & it fell like a vial
of melted lead into my heart, my heart so
deep in my chest. She will have to do it now,
we have presented her with a world,
whose spectres take shapes before her eyes
have fully focust, poor voyager! For joy
she brings us every morning we exchange
an accelerating series of shocks. We are together
cannibals of her spirit, we feast to nurture
our tired bodies, turning music to shit, a shock
felt numbly here & radiating to collisions
at the rim of space. You dont believe me?
See her eyes when first she wakes. A visible
tyrant of light yanks their traces, demanding
they stride apace.

IX

        Then cannibal I will be —
her father. & I cant even teach her love,
but loose the horses, let a ghost ride &
call him loving, turn her away finally &
soothe her with a merry-go-round. That music
will disgust her in time, it rings & rings,
& I will instruct her of gold & gold
bedevillings, I will toil to win her trust,
& we will fall where we will rust
& watch the golden horses prancing by.

X

So fall will come
& winter too,
& she will hear
her first tight shoe

& she will wear
the seasons round
& watch the summers
wear me down.

XI

Thea, never read my lines, love your mother,
love your father, distrust circles, reach
this way & that. Remember how you can
the afternoon a bird came to sit at your shoulder
& let me remember how I dropt my game
to fly to your side, protecting your eyes.
Accept no promise from the mountains,
I have never seen your face before, & when
I leave you I will leave you time.
Forgive me the light that fades not fast away,
forgive me the continuous feast
we make from your remembered day.

DESERT ELM

I

I woke, & woke again, to see her smiling
at me, & turned to find soft sleep in the
green pillow.

Later in the day she said what were you
dreaming, you were smiling in your sleep,
but again it was my sleep, though I have never
said that.

Later I felt the pain three times inside
my left arm, driving the red car, & I remembered, I had dreamt that I too had had
my heart attack.

Attack, I didnt mean that when I told her,
sitting now on my lap, it was simply all
I could remember of my dream & thinking,
of course, but I am nearly thirty years
younger than him.

He finally had his on the green grass of
the golf course, how mundane, how it
filled my mother's voice with unwonted
fear, to be telling this to me.

I thought of a rock, not quite round, tonight, reading H.D. on the old age of the
professor, a rock, not quite round, beginning to crack, it will crumble, will
I know this earth.

II

The earth he made me on, we dug into
side by side, has not long been there,
has been carried there by the glacier,
all rocks & all round rocks, all stones
rolled together.

We toiled among the stones, that rattling
sound is my earth, where I grew up looking like him. There was some light falling always into the valley, always blue,
the blue that hovers over heat, a blue
I saw cooling the Adriatic shore.

It is the blue fading in his eyes, they
are not startling blue, it is the family
colour I never got, they are not bright
blue but fading into a transparency you
will notice only if you are watching
closely, I mean within a few feet.

They found a desert & made it bloom, made
it green, but even the fairways seen from
across the valley are under a blue haze,
the smoke of space it seemed on high summer days, not a cloud in the sky, no mote
in that eye.

The earth is not brown but grey, grey of
stones, the flat stones round to the eye
looking straight down.

III

I never saw him attack anything but a
baseball, a golf ball, his own records,
to be beaten despite his getting older,
to compete satisfactorily with himself.
That is why he never rebuked her, he is
more pure than I.

He said hold the hammer at the handle's
end, for leverage, not because he was a
science teacher, because he knew how to
do it, full out, not thinking or rather
thinking wide open, down the lines of
energy.

He had those muscles you can see under
the skin, the large vein down the middle
of his biceps I never had, I didnt get
the blue eyes or that, & not the straight
nose, I would perhaps never have broken
it then.

He is associated with no colour, no colour
clothes or car or house, he would as soon
eat a peach as an apple. I think of the
apple splitting in half as some can make
it between their hands, as he could likely
do that, & it is white.

In the last two years his hair is thin
& one may see between them, & they are
white. His slacks were white below the
purple blazer, & worn twice a month.

IV

Rounding the bases his neck became red as
a turkey's but it was a home run, every
one like me has to see his father do that
once, fearing his father is like him, not
as good.

Red as a turkey neck, his eyes bulging,
his heart already something to frighten
the young boy, was it something she said
as this other says now to me playing my
guerrilla ball, I dont want you collapsing
& dying on the field. It is a playing field,
I say, I can feel my blood running red
under the skin.

I tell him about it whenever I can, my
average, joking as if I am my team & he is
his, & sometime we must come together,
clasp & both of us, win. He was his mother's
first child, I was my mother's first child,
& after us came just all the rest, the
bases cleared already.

But he didnt get it done till a quarter
century later, he lay they say on the fresh
cut grass, all the red gone from under the
skin of his face, pale, these pale blue
eyes looking for her?

In my dream I thought of course, I too,
what will I take up when too old to round
the bases, what crimson driver.

V

I thought of a rock, not quite round
sticking half out of the earth where I
would put the ladder's foot. In a hurry,
without patience to place it safely, to
be up that tree & working.

& working. Never half as fast as he could
do it, but in some ways inheriting his
quiet efficiency & turning it to grace.
He said he could never play second base
& I found it the easiest position, bending
over occasionally to pick stones off the
ground.

Even this summer, a month before his fall,
he pickt twenty pounds while I pickt
eleven, just more than half & I am more
than half at last, thirty-seven, moving
around to the other half of the tree,
but someone guesst, that is under the
ground, the root system.

A tree, growing downward as I dreamed I
would or desperately hoped I would, to
become this child again, never having the
nerve or wit, age four, to follow that to

its home, from one hundred back to the
seed, & then what. A new lease on life?
For him?

The earthly tree grows downward, we do it
after all, bypassing the womb, back where
we came from, down the rabbit hole on the
golf course, above the shade of the old
cherry tree.

VI

General knowledges are those knowledges
that idiots possess. What words would you
use to characterize your relationship with
your parents. Scratchy tweed pants they
provided for sunday school. I remember because of my legs. They look now like his
legs, shorts he wears at the golf course,
no embarrassment, he has come this far,
what are they to him?

Prophecy is finally simple & simply more
interesting than characterization. We are
not characters, we devise characters. I
sat as still as possible, the backs of my

knees held forward from the hard curved
wood. Those pants were never worn out,
though they belonged unused to some uncle
first.

His white slacks hung for two weeks in the
closet we'd built some years earlier, he ˙
took them out two Tuesdays each month. A
lifetime uses few such garments. Who wears
the pants in this family is no sociological
question. Prophecy is no answer. If you
need an answer go make up a question &
leave me alone without it.

He has those muscles you can see under the
skin, the calf muscle like mine tending toward the other, inside the line of shin
bone. I see his lines every morning in the
mirror.

VII

I woke & again I woke, to find her smiling
at me, & turned to return to soft sleep
in the green pillow. A tree, growing downward as I dreamed we all would or hoped

we would, against my god or what they
gave me as my god, their god, given them
against their will, we punish the generation that succeeds us.

Did I mean to say he did that. No, he
never tried to bend my life, never stood
between me & the sun, this tree grew where
the seed fell. A new lease on life? For
him? In the thick dark forest the trees
grow tall before they extend wings. Tall
green pillow.

They found a desert & made it bloom, made
it green, but even the trees feel blue
smoke curling among their branches, the
smoke that holds away the frost, the early
message that fills our heart with ice,
lovely to taste fresh from the branch,
but it doesnt travel well. All stones
rolled together, long enough & they will
all be dust, hanging in the air over our
blue lakes.

Prophecy is finally simple, & simply a
pair of eyes thru which the blue of the
sky travels, an observation thru a lens.

VIII

Staring straight into his eyes for the
first time, I see the blue, a sky with
some puffy clouds many miles away.
Step into the nearby field, over the sill,
into footprints that disappear as I step
into them, into the blue sky that is not
above but straight in front of me. Straight
eyes, in all the photographs, & in one old
brown Kodak print of the family assembled
I look into his oval eyes & see inside
them a man walking backward, out of his
footsteps.

My eyes are brown, walking inside them
would be moving over burned grass on low
hills. They found a desert & made it bloom.
I move closer, zooming into his eyes &
find the first aperture completely filled
with one petal of a blue flower, a close-
up of a star weeping in surrender to the
earth, a tear, Aurora weeping helplessly
on the edge of the Blue Nile.

He's no sun of mine, I never stood between
him & the brightness, the mistakes I make
will live as long as these ovals stay open.
I walkt into his open eye, over the sill
& saw two enormous black holes in the sky.
A voice came thru a nose & reduced them
to personality. I had never said the word
poetry without a funny accent.

IX

Men who love wisdom should acquaint themselves with a great many particulars.
Cutting the crisp apple with a French knife
I saw that the worm had lived in the core
& chewed his way out, something I've seen
a thousand times & never understood & while
I'm looking he's on the other side of the
green tree picking. One two one two, the
wisdom of the tree filling his picking bag,
its weight strapt over his shoulders. He
showed me, you cross the straps like this
& keep it high. Get above the apples & look
down at them.

& I still do it wrong, reaching up, picking with sore arms, strain rather than wisdom filling me not the bag. He said the
safest step on the ladder is the top, he
was trying to get me up, & always right,
this one I have learned & Saturday I was
on the top step picking apples, wanting
someone to advise. That is how one becomes
acquainted, working to gather.

It could be a woman but is it a woman. Is
it a woman you can work together with, is
it a woman you know doesnt feel the particulars as you do, they are apples, not the
picking of them, the filling. She has been
without a man for years, she offers ladders,
tools, bags for the apples. You want someone to advise to be him, but do it silently
knowing your expertise is somehow, known.

x

I did not see him lying on the grass, I
may as well have been under the ground,
perhaps entangled in the tree growing downward, an earth. His earth, our particular
earth, as it sifts back & forth, composing

like dust on a piano. The piano is black
but where it has been rubbed it is brown.
He never sat at a piano, only an old black
typewriter with round keys, making faint
words.

So faint they barely heard him. It was August & the grass dry, the thin words rose
like a tree into the air, lightly, as blue
as the thin smoke hanging over the green
fairway. It has nothing to do with justice.
He spent thousands of hours in those trees
picking pennies for me, this day he was
knocking them into a hole, I'm glad to hear
that.

In the ocean light of the ward window his
eyes are barely blue & deep in his head
like my daughter's. He woke again to see
me smiling at him, his head straight in
the pillow, a rock nearly round. In the
desert the rocks simply lie upon each other
on the ground, a tree is overturned out
of the ground, its shallow widespread roots
coiled around small rocks. By these fruits
we measure our weight & days.

DO SINK

1.

When I have fears that I
may cease to be
open to pain that shines
wet on the side of a gold
fish in my own, I thought,
pond

      I ought to forget
comfort, forget family
history, drive a black sedan
over thin prairie roads
looking for a town even
my mother does not believe
was ever there

          knowing
pain is not colour, not value
but condition, the cost
of starting a damned life
in the first place, where no
thinking man ever was.

2.

Before my pen has
gleaned my teeming brain
the vehicle of forget all this
piece by piece will pull up
from behind, an unremembered
cousin at the wheel

                        coloured
like the car and beautiful
in a tailored shirt, forget
that and that and that thing
you've not quite recalled,
take my hand

                   & souls of poets
long since gone sit down to sing
with your family, did you think
you could just grow those
upper arms, wait for a bus, and get
whisked away beyond pain?

3.

Before high-piled books,
in charactery this fool
scribes his day, walks the town
as if new to the job without
rising from his desk, a black car
parked in back

        with orange cats
coiled on the warm hood, his team
of familiars, his destiny, nine
lifetimes prepared hopelessly, this
idiot with a black pen writes
and yet writes

        with ginger
in his shadowed heart, protected
from the sun and its rays, the
measure of the year a few lines
that will last longer than a cherry
tree bird's song.

4.

Driving a dusty black sedan
over flimsy prairie roads,
he feels his eyes and mind's machine
hold like rich garners
the full ripened grain, the
dark void of night

                    somewhere
high behind him, while family
never met will rush from ground
like wheat into a lovely maiden's
hand, her picture now the reverse
of our currency

                  dropped from our
fingers faster and faster as we age,
dirt from our skin piled into heaps
to rival these small prairie hills, loam
to grow a grandmother, obfuscate
a self.

5.

When I behold, upon the night's
starred face, a gold sheen, I know
my eyes are old beyond their desire,
two aged deer as dull as the surface
of this pond

       I contemplate
falling into, when I behold
no star's reflection on that face
I hate the books piled high
that told me heaven was
what we worked for, fame
was love

       deferred, a family
wider than a suburb firmament,
a story we must aid the telling of,
we must edit with our
failing breath.

6.

Huge cloudy symbols of a high
romance in the night sky shimmer,
images of satisfied self-murder
haunt one's eyes inside the windshield
on the prairie, drive he said, everyone
insane

     with melodious chuckle
in strings heard from rear speakers,
laughter beside a dark road dangerous
& narrow under starlight, families
emerging from hard soil, weed roots
sliding from their shoulders

                weak
from disuse, exactly what the thrush,
could he have spoken, would have said,
an observant eye in available light, a
relative bird awake when one is nearly
asleep at the wheel.

7.

I'm driving this black sedan
too swiftly over rutted prairie roads
and think I may never live to trace
my DNA another generation
down the route of fate, oh damn
such maunderings

                come upon so early
in the dying business, before my pen
has gleaned a thing worth harvesting,
or so one says every year, and considers
a grandmother who likely never wrote at all
save misspelled letters to her sister

lost to the south, caught in a draught
no one could have expected, deep
in another family, wild shoeless brothers
with big noses, my kin, my semblables,
too dear to keep in memory, in a line
that grows longer as we walk it.

8.

Driving under dark prairie clouds
I confuse their shadows with
the magic hand of chance, lose
all trace of grandparents to the geography,
the ground converted

                    in the vehicular
mind into latitudes, for instance,
of mortality, no matter the voices
alongside the road, no matter the urgings
of the season, haunting is haunting, dying
is less exciting as it goes

                 along, looking
for whatever it looks for, chromosomes,
colours of late seasons, cruel anemones, perhaps
sprouting out of literature with comic face,
comic mice under those nearby leaves,
I think they are, racing by.

9.

      And when I feel, fair
creature of an hour, brought up
so rudely from the earth, that I
will never see you plain, your whispering
by the roadside like the night breeze
in thistles

      seems to propel this black
vehicle, no star's reflection on its back,
an almost unseen shark in the gloom,
and in its belly a tiring brain that wants only
some abandoned town you lived in
too young to know its name

         and then dead
too soon to hear of mine, oh a sentence
can never be as confused as our line, the
unknowing all along it, the progeny
suffering in silence some pain for one actual,
for the next a story being told.

10.

I'm scared to death that I shall never
look upon thee more clear than
I do tonight, dark creature of a time
long past my memory, long past the desire
of my mother's recollection, who never
heard these roadside ditches sing

                                 this song
like thistles, like music scribed by pens
gleaning brains we would never recognize
even were their headstones to be found
in that pine-bordered plot in the middle
of the bald-headed

                      where a black sedan
parked in westering sunlight while this
lorn grandson walked hopeless and lost
on his DNA's purported earth again, you
nowhere to be found inside that square, only
encountered in the roadside's bright dirge.

II.

Locked inside this heavy car, I
will never have relish in the faery
power known to the unknown who
walked this way in a musical past, never
ride the vehicle invisible beyond desire,
never remember

        where my share of
molecules might fetch up, D for desire,
N for Never, and A for a beginning
we all have honestly missed, watching
intently as we can the roadside slippage,
the willows in the wind

        that is only
main component of our song, oh what ears
we waste on one another's plaints, oh
what hours we cast aside while our dearest
family dies in other arms, oh how late
we come to realize or not.

12.

When I perceive the prairie beside the road
as a pond of unreflecting love —
then on the sore far from this dark
the night sky falls to wrap those quick
golden shapes

                    that swim like thought
where we seek no mother's mother, here
beneath the still wheels of this dark sedan
are bones enough, unbending below
their burden of invisible earth, stones
caught in the arms of soil

                            some tried
to instruct us has always been the base
of our being, while we, riders
of pneumatic spin, cast our loyalty
to an idea, God is Love, Mother
is Queen of Earth, Dian of Heaven
and whatever that is out there.

13.

I remember this night, getting out
of the car to wait: in the reputed centre
of the wide world I stand alone, and think
like a sheen of gold-sided fish, flitting
into the dark, no stars in this crown, no
supreme darkness

            to see them in, a voice
by the side of the road is only the weather,
no stone marks a grave if it is here,
the dying business is not tidy, ruts in the road
are direction, not aid, the end of light
is partly darkness only

            given to grandsons
who cannot turn their eyes to look inward,
and will forget the time they tried, have fears
that themselves will cease to be, when suns
rise and bring partial light, gold at first, a
flash of lesser metal, a day.

14

When I have fear that eyes may
cease to be upon me, looking only through
what seems to be there, here, in the centre
of the shadowed earth nearly flat with age,
oh then what seems to me a mother's mother
is only the mother

               of these late thoughts,
what vehicle brings us to this halt, what spectre
carriage with what geography implied, oh
let me remain outside, above the maternal ground
of being, below the dark clouds of seeming,
inside any out there is

                 relative to what
there is not, let me start the engine and release
anything, the clutch, the earthlike hold of bones,
release the music of the roadside ditches, back
let me go, let me rouse my fancied kin and think
till song and pain to nothingness do sink.

July–August 1991

CREDITS

The poems in this book were originally published in the following editions (listed by order of appearance of poems in this volume):

Points on the Grid (Toronto: Contact Press, 1964)
The Man in Yellow Boots (Mexico: Ediciones El Corno, 1965)
Sitting in Mexico (Calgary: Beaver Kosmos, 1965)
The Silver Wire (Kingston: Quarry Press, 1966)
The Gangs of Kosmos (Toronto: House of Anansi, 1969)
Rocky Mountain Foot (Toronto: McClelland and Stewart, 1971)
George, Vancouver (Kitchener: Weed/Flower, 1970)
Geneve (Toronto: Coach House, 1971)
Autobiology (Vancouver: New Star, 1972)
Curious (Toronto: Coach House, 1973)
In the Flesh (Toronto: McClelland and Stewart, 1974)
The Concrete Island (Montreal: Vehicule, 1977)
Another Mouth (Toronto: McClelland and Stewart, 1979)
Smoking Mirror (Edmonton: Longspoon, 1982)
West Window: Selected Poetry (Toronto: General, 1982)
Seventy-One Poems for People (Red Deer: Red Deer College, 1985)
Delayed Mercy and Other Poems (Toronto: Coach House, 1986)
A, You're Adorable (Ottawa: Above Ground, 1998)
Urban Snow (Vancouver: Talon, 1992)
Blonds on Bikes (Ottawa: Above Ground, 1997)
His Life (Toronto: ECW, 2000)
Some Writers (Calgary: House Press, 2001)
The Catch (Toronto: McClelland and Stewart, 1976)
Do Sink (Vancouver: Pomflit, 1992)

George Bowering was born in 1935 and brought up in the Okanagan Valley of British Columbia, where he bought his first book of poems at Frank's Poolhall. He began his writing career as a sports reporter, indulging his love of basketball and baseball, but soon turned to poetry and fiction. Over the past forty years he has published over forty books. Bowering has won the Governor-General's Award twice — first for poetry, with *Rocky Mountain Foot* and *The Gangs of Kosmos* — and once for fiction. He has also won the Canadian Authors' Association Award for Poetry and the bpNichol Chapbook Award for Poetry. He has received many accolades, including honourary doctorates from the universities of British Columbia and Western Ontario. In 2002, in recognition of his extraordinary accomplishments, Bowering was appointed Canada's Poet Laureate. He was made an Officer of the Order of Canada in 2003. He received the Order of British Columbia in 2004.